MOTOR SPORT IN THE 20s

MOTOR SPORT IN THE 20s

A.B. DEMAUS

ALAN SUTTON
1989

ALAN SUTTON PUBLISHING
BRUNSWICK ROAD · GLOUCESTER · UK

ALAN SUTTON PUBLISHING INC
WOLFEBORO · NEW HAMPSHIRE · USA

First published 1989

British Library Cataloguing in Publication Data

Demaus, A.B.
Motor sport in the 20s.
1. Great Britain. Motor sports 1920–1930
I. Title
796.7

ISBN 0-86299-599-X

Library of Congress Cataloging in Publication Data
applied for

*Cover photograph: R.F. Summers clips the lower S-bend in his
Aston Martin at Shelsley Walsh, July 1924*

Typesetting and origination by
Alan Sutton Publishing Limited
Printed in Great Britain.

CONTENTS

ACKNOWLEDGEMENTS

The author is greatly indebted to the many people who have encouraged him in his love of motor cars for very many years and who have given him the benefit of their knowledge and experience.

In particular he would like to thank Geoffrey Boston, Mrs Agnes Gripper and Mrs Geoffrey Moore from whose family albums he has drawn extensively in selecting the photographs.

PICTURE CREDITS

The following sources of individual photographs are gratefully acknowledged: J. Ahern and D. Irvine (13 inset, 16, 17, 18, 77, 78 lower, 97, 98 upper, 99); Dr J. Alderson (3 upper); P. Bartlett (111 upper); P.T. Beardsell (72 lower); G.S. Boston (11, 25, 26, 29 upper, 31, 33 upper, 47 upper, 50 lower, 56 upper, 66, 74, 104, 105, 106, 107, 108, 110 lower); D.P. Brogden (23 lower); Classic Photographs (86 lower); M. Crosthwaite (67); The late A. I. Dick (78 upper, 80); M.H. Flower (64, 65); The late W. Gibbs (19 lower, 39 upper, 58 upper, 69 upper, 70 lower, 71, 75 inset, 76, 79, 87); Mrs A.G. Gripper (7 lower, 9, 15, 42 lower, 75 upper, 83, 84, 86 upper, 91, 94 lower, 96 inset, 100); S.P.R. Hall (8 upper, 12 upper, 85); Mrs J. Helsby (47 lower); Dr T. Houlding/The Bentley Drivers Club (6 inset); R. Howard (1, 2, 19 upper, 20, 21, 22, 23, 24, 116); J. Martin (40, 57); Mrs G. Moore (3 inset, 30, 33 lower, 34, 36, 38, 39 lower, 41, 42 upper, 43, 48, 49, 51 upper, 52, 53, 92 upper, 109 upper); A.J.A. Pearson (51 lower); Mrs P. Perrin (10 lower); C. Posthumus (62 upper); J. Pritchard (14 inset); Mrs C. Sgonina (28 upper, 56 lower, 110 upper, 111 lower); N.W. Slatter (96 lower); Dr W.E. Snell (28 lower); W.H. Summers (13 upper, 44, 46, 68, 72 upper, 73 lower); G.H. Taylor (58 lower, 59, 60, 61, 63 upper); D. Williams (102, 109 lower). The remaining photographs are from the author's own collection.

LIST OF ABBREVIATIONS

BARC	Brooklands Automobile Racing Club
BRDC	British Racing Drivers Club
cc	cubic capacity
fwd	front wheel drive
ftd	fastest time of the day
hp	horse power
JCC	Junior Car Club
MC	Motor Club
mph	miles per hour
ohc	overhead camshaft
o/s	off side
rpm	revolutions per minute
sv	side valve

INTRODUCTION

Motoring for sport — that is to say in a situation where there is a competitive element — is almost as old as the motor car itself. The eminent motoring historian G.N. Georgano remarked in his Introduction to *A Motor Racing Camera, 1894–1916*,* that 'competition lies in the heart of every man'. Thus the invention of the motor car provided a new vehicle, in the widest sense of the word, for that competitive nature just as the invention of the bicycle had done in its time.

In the very earliest days of the car its very novelty, mechanical unreliability and temperamental nature invested each and every journey with a sense of competition so that to complete the journey was in itself a challenge. But to leave it at that largely ignores the competitive element in most people. It is not enough merely to have achieved the basic objective of taking the vehicle from A to B. Rather, there is the urge to go farther or faster than one's fellows, to impose greater tests and difficulties that have to be overcome, again preferably when pitted against the efforts of rival human beings.

The European continent, particularly France, fostered the earliest motor competitions. The great Paris–Rouen Trial of 1894 attracted a large entry and sowed the seeds of the legendary 'Town to Town' races of the turn of the century that in turn led to the Grand Prix of later years. Success in competition brought fame to the cars and their drivers and such success was used by the car makers as valuable publicity. The awesome 'giant' motor cars from the 'heroic age' of motor racing bore little resemblance to the more humdrum vehicles in everyday use on the road, but would a Le Mans Jaguar or Ferrari be driven on the roads of today? Nevertheless it remains true

* David & Charles, 1976.

that success with such cars in the competitions of today still brings rewards to cars, drivers and manufacturers, all of which reflect on the sales of the more mundane cars that the public can buy.

Many factors go into making up a sport of any kind. They may be somewhat arbitrarily divided into the human and the material. The higher the quality of the material – the car and its accessories – the better the chance of the human element being successful in competition. But the human factor, as always, holds the key: a poor or average driver may theoretically have a better chance of success if his car is in all respects, mechanical and technical, the best, but a highly skilled driver may well overcome the disadvantages of an inferior machine to gain success over a driver of lesser calibre in a superior machine. As always there is the fickle element of luck which so often upsets all calculations.

As motor sport developed it cast up its 'great' cars and drivers that became famous from the vastly wider field of amateurs who were in it for the fun and without the financial and technical backing of motor manufacturers or the sponsorship of the petrol, oil, tyre and accessory suppliers.

By the 1920s the Grand Prix, the track events, the sprint speed trials, the speed hill-climbs, the sand racing, the reliability trials were all well established. The Great War had brought a hugely increased mechanical awareness to the nation as a whole. Those young men who survived it were joined by the many, too young to have sampled motor sport before 1914, eager to take part now that peace was restored. As the war years receded an ever increasing number of motor sporting events came into being up and down the length of the country as this pleasure-seeking and motor-orientated decade rolled on.

In selecting the photographs it has been the deliberate aim to emphasise the part played by the keen amateur in the sport. The faces of the famous and their cars do appear from time to time, but by and large it is those who competed for the sheer enjoyment who feature most. If certain makes of cars appear very frequently, as indeed they do, it is because they were the makes that produced the successful sports cars of the time, a very small proportion of the many makes (most of them names that have long passed into oblivion) that could be seen on the roads of Britain in that exciting decade.

The selection of the photographs aims to bring out the charming informality of the sport at that time. Cars were almost invariably driven on the road to and from the events, often in various states of 'undress'. Particularly in the smaller clubs the organization was friendly and informal. Regulations there had to be, of course, but they were interpreted as liberally as possible without giving cause for complaint or a sense of injustice.

For many the 1920s were the heyday of motor sport. The overriding impression of the decade was a sense of enjoyment and fun among kindred competitive spirits.

Zborowski's chain-drive 'monster' *Chitty-Chitty-Bang-Bang I* with which he made many Brooklands appearances is seen outside its Higham lair in 1922

BROOKLANDS

Possibly as many words have been written about the Brooklands track as the total number of miles travelled on it by the many hundreds of drivers who raced there during its active existence. This surely must be some reflection on the importance that Brooklands holds in the history of motor sport and in the affections of racing enthusiasts.

During the 1920s a number of motor racing events of major importance were inaugurated there. In 1921 came the Junior Car Club's (JCC) 200-Miles Race for light cars which was so successful that it was repeated annually until 1928, the last year in which this classic event was held at Brooklands, though it emerged again elsewhere ten years later.

The Essex Motor Club pulled off a notable 'first' on 22 May 1922 when they laid on the first 'Royal' Race Meeting at the track, attended by HRH the Duke of York. The Earl of Athlone, in his Foreword to the official souvenir programme, remarked: 'This is the first Brooklands race meeting under Royal patronage, and its importance to the motor industry cannot be over-estimated . . .'. *The Motor Owner* published a well illustrated souvenir programme stating that the proceeds of the meeting would be donated to the Industrial Welfare Society and the Middlesex Hospital, both organizations of which the duke was president. The duke had also entered two motor cycles, a Douglas and a Trump-Anzani, in the motor cycle events of the day.

The first ever British Grand Prix came to Brooklands in 1926 and was held there again the following year, victory in both years going to Delage. Further innovations were the Six Hours Race for sports cars, inspired by the famous Le Mans 24-Hour events, and introduced by the Essex Motor Club. The Brooklands

Capt Alastair Miller in the vast 200 hp Benz which was said to have been Hindenburg's staff car in the First World War. He appears to have the track to himself in this 1928 shot

Automobile Racing Club (BARC) took over the organization of this event in 1929 after the demise of the
Essex Motor Club. Another 1929 innovation was the
JCC's Double-Twelve, even more in the Le Mans
idiom but of necessity 'split' because night racing was
not permitted at Brooklands. Not to be outdone the
British Racing Drivers Club (BRDC) put on the 500-
Miles Race as another 1929 newcomer, a race which
was destined to become one of the major classics of
the following decade.

Capt H.R. Hazelhurst's Salmson at speed on the banking at a Surbiton MC meeting in 1928

These were the highlights, but throughout the
1920s Brooklands was the scene of countless smaller
club events such as the JCC's High Speed Trials,
introduced in 1925, which used some of the interlinking roads within the embrace of the circuit so as to
combine 'road' and 'track' elements in the event. Also
throughout the year the track was used by manufacturers and individuals for testing and record
breaking, including the record for the ascent of the
famous Test Hill.

The late Whitney Straight, one of the most successful drivers on the track, wrote in 1971 that by the
closure of Brooklands in 1939 the amateur lost most.
A very true reflection as for every 'star' who won the
big races there must have been a hundred amateurs,
just as keen if not as skilled, for whom Brooklands
provided exactly the friendly and enthusiastic 'all of
one family' atmosphere in which they and their sport
flourished.

Above: The autumn of 1921 saw the inauguration of the highly successful 200-Miles Races staged by the Junior Car Club. Some of the field of thirty-eight starters in that first of the series can be seen here on the track. The car in the centre is the Aston Martin driven by Zborowski/ Gallop.
Inset: All smiles as Capt 'Archie' Frazer-Nash wins the 1100 cc class with his GN in the very first 200-Miles Race at Brooklands on 22 October 1921. His average speed was 71.54 mph

Above: Stripes and pipes. 'Bertie' Kensington Moir's dazzle-painted Straker-Squire which had a successful career in his hands is seen at a 1922 event. Note the parallel 'organ pipe' exhaust system giving one pipe per cylinder

Below: Pictured in the paddock at the same meeting is N.F. Holder's slim pre-war Vauxhall fitted with an E-type 30/98 engine said to have been bored 1 mm oversize. Nicknamed the *Blue Streak*, the car lapped at 83.56 mph in the Private Competitors' Handicap

Inset: A Crouch moves up to the start line for one of the August Bank Holiday races, 1922. These unusual cars had a two-cylinder 1,100cc engine at the rear. A sister car, driven by J.W. Tollady, lapped at over 82 mph in 1922

Below: Pictured in the paddock in August 1922, this slender and immaculate Horstman was a light car built in Bath. Various proprietory engines were used, the most successful being the well-proven 1,496cc, sv Anzani

Above: Here one of the Aston Martin track cars comes in for interested scrutiny. As was often the case at Brooklands, a cowl disguised and streamlined the radiator

Inset: F.C. Clement in one of the early experimental 3-litre Bentleys, Exp 2, in 1920/21. The car exhibits several component features that were altered in the production cars and is fitted with the old body from Exp 1

Above: H.V. Barlow in the massive 21,504cc chain-driven Benz which could lap at over 114 mph. It was one of a number of old racing cars of pre-war vintage that, suitably modified, saw a new lease of life at Brooklands in the early 1920s

The works A.C. racing models of the early 1920s had bronze cylinder heads, a single chain-driven ohc and sixteen valves. They also carried very pretty aluminium bodies, slender and nicely streamlined. In this posed shot J.A. Joyce is seated in one of the single-seater models

Another monster was the 350 hp V-12 Sunbeam used successfully for land speed record attempts by Kenelm Lee Guiness (seen at the wheel in 1922) and later by Malcolm Campbell who achieved 150.766 mph at Pendine in 1925

Capt 'Archie' Frazer-Nash, pipe in mouth as usual, with his GN, in the paddock at the meeting in August 1922. With various permutations on the sports GN theme, he was one of the most successful drivers in all types of event in the early 1920s

W.D. Hawkes' Anzani-engined Morgan with shaft drive ohc to each cylinder is seen at the pits in the 1922 200-Miles Race. Hawkes retired with a blown engine after lapping at 88 mph

Above: The successful 200-Miles Race was held for the second time on 19 August 1922. The 1100cc race was held separately from the 1½-litre event, the smaller cars starting at the earlier hour of 8.30 a.m. Seen here is the winning car in the 1100cc race, Robert Benoist's Salmson No.5. His average speed was 81.88 mph. In the foreground is a 30/98 Vauxhall

Below: If the Leyland Eight was dubbed 'The lion of Olympia' when it made its debut at the 1920 show, then undoubtedly its designer J.G. Parry Thomas became 'The lion of Brooklands'. He is seen here with one of his creations on the banking at Brooklands

Above: G.S. Boston portrayed in his stripped 30/98 Vauxhall in September 1923. This most versatile car was used as everyday transport, for all types of sprint events, for lengthy continental tours and, as here, on the track

Inset: For the 1923 200-Miles Race Fiat entered two of their very advanced 1½-litre 2-ohc supercharged cars for Charles Salamano and Malcolm Campbell to drive. Great things were expected of them but both retired. This is Salamano's car which caught fire on the twelfth lap

The first 200-Miles Race was a one, two, three victory for the Talbot-Darracq in the 1½-litre class. They won again in 1922, also taking third place. In 1924, now termed just Darracq, they again pulled off a one, two, three victory. Here is Kenelm Lee Guinness in the winning car. His top speed was 102.27 mph

Left: A close-up of Miss Henrietta M. Lister in her mottled aluminium-bodied sv Aston Martin. A ballerina and artist, she entered and most frequently drove this car successfully at Brooklands in the 1924 to 1928 period. The car still survives today in appreciative ownership

Above: The start of the Private Competitors' Handicap, Whitsun Meeting, 1924. Among the varied assortment of cars the one asterisked is R.F. Summers' Aston Martin. An Alvis and an Austin are first away

Inset: Both W. Urquhart Dykes, whose Alvis is seen here in action in the JCC Spring Meeting on 30 April 1927, and his wife were consistent performers with Alvis cars in the mid- to late 1920s

Above: C.M. Harvey's fwd Alvis is in the foreground of this start line for the 200-Miles Race held on 26 September 1925. He was flagged off 45 min after the winner crossed the line, having covered sixty-four laps

Inset: J.G. Parry Thomas, in characteristic sloppy woollen pullover, in conversation with A.V. Ebblewhite ('Ebby'), starter and RAC timekeeper, beside one of the Talbot Specials in 1926. This was the second year in which the JCC had insisted that all entries in its major events be termed 'Specials'

The first British Grand Prix was staged at Brooklands on 7 August 1926. A team of three straight-eight 1½-litre Delages and a team of straight-eight 1½-litre Talbots were the most favoured contestants, while Campbell's Bugatti was also a serious contender. The Delage exhaust system cooked their drivers unmercifully on a hot day. Here Sénechal is seen in the winning Delage. His team mate Benoist took third place behind Campbell's Bugatti

Above: Major F.B. Halford's very advanced 1½-litre Halford Special leads two rivals round the marker barrel in the JCC Spring Meeting, 30 April 1927. The engine featured an exhaust-driven turbo-supercharger which was mounted on an Aston Martin chassis. The car was acquired by Capt G.E.T. Eyston when Halford gave up racing

Inset: R. Plunkett-Greene, friend and associate of Evelyn Waugh, brings his Frazer Nash up the straight in the same event. He entered his Frazer Nash for the 1928 200-Miles Race, but was one of sixteen drivers to retire

Above: J.S.H. Wilson's Gordon England Austin Seven at the spring meeting of 30 April 1927. He finished in sixth place in the JCC's Junior Grand Prix over fifteen laps

Inset: The JCC had inaugurated the High Speed Trial in 1925. It became very popular and lasted well into the 1930s. Part of the interlinking roads within the track were used and here a Bugatti, pursued by a Lea-Francis, joins the road section on 18 June 1927

The road section used in these JCC events provided some narrow, poorly surfaced track, with sharp corners and included a dash through the Members' Tunnel and around the road to the Members' Bridge. Here we see Booty's Aston Martin leading a Salmson and an A.C. in the same event

Above: Eyston's Aston Martin leads in this shot of a Surbiton Motor Club race in 1928. This car had been delivered new to Capt G.E.T. Eyston in 1924. By this time it had acquired an Anzani engine and was usually driven by his brother Basil

Below: The Wellsteed Special, seen here at the August Bank Holiday Meeting in 1928, driven by Cyril Paul, was a private modification of a Morris Oxford. The chassis was liberally drilled the suspension altered and the radiator cowled. Paul managed to get the Wellsteed to lap at 78.43 mph

The various GP Sunbeam racing cars had a long career at Brooklands, appearing at various times in the hands of a number of well-known drivers. Not as well-known as some, perhaps, E.L. Bouts is seen here in 1928

Mrs W.B. Scott, one of the most successful women drivers to appear at Brooklands, is seen here in her Bugatti. She won a four-lap ladies race with this car in one of the Surbiton MCs 1928 events

Above: Kaye Don's Bugatti leads a Lea-Francis in a 1928 Surbiton MC event. Don was a very versatile driver who had started racing with motor cycles. He drove many different cars in the late '20s and early '30s and was an unsuccessful contender for the World Land Speed Record with the Sunbeam-built *Silver Bullet*

Below: The lines of Urquhart Dykes' much raced Alvis show up well in this shot of him in action in 1928

Another Edwardian giant still active on the track at an advanced age was this 10½-litre Fiat, seen with R. Warde at the wheel in 1928.

The 1910 10½-litre Fiat (Warde) and 5-litre Delage II which was driven on this occasion by 'J. Taylor', alias Philip Turner, in close company, 1928.

Above: Delage II ('Taylor') and Kaye Don's Sunbeam at speed, July 1928. 'Taylor' won the Surrey Senior Long Handicap at 111.92 mph, 20 yd ahead of Don's Sunbeam. Delage II survives and is still raced today

Inset: The Birkin/Harcourt-Wood supercharged 4½-litre Bentley passing a Thomas Special 'flat-iron' in the BRDC 500-Miles Race on 12 October 1929. Oddly enough both cars caught fire later in the race

Above: A general view of the start as drivers sprint for their cars Le Mans style in the BARC Six-Hours Race held on 29 June 1929. Riley, fwd Alvis and Lea-Francis cars can be seen in the foreground

Inset: 'Old No.1' 6½-litre Bentley of S.C.H. Davis and Clive Dunfee leads a string of cars headed by John Pole's giant 17,850cc Mercedes. The Bentley put up the fastest lap at 126.09 mph in this, the first of the 500-Miles Races

SPEED HILL-CLIMBS

At the start of the decade the same situation continued as had existed prior to the Great War: there were a number of well-established events held on public roads where, over a distance of perhaps a kilometre or a mile, on a reasonable gradient and with one or two bends of a not too acute nature, cars could compete against the clock over the measured distance. The road surfaces often varied considerably and in most cases would be considered execrable by today's standards.

The number of events increased markedly as new venues were found that fulfilled the basic requirements. A certain degree of remoteness from large centres of population was desirable in order to minimize the effects of noise and crowds and, indeed, to increase the likelihood of friendly co-operation by the police authorities who had to turn a blind eye to what was, strictly speaking, the illegal act of running a speed event on a public road.

Although some degree of attention was paid in the printed regulations for these events as to the well-being and safety of spectators, helped by the marshals acting for the promoting clubs, in practice it was often a case of 'each man for himself'. Spectators crowded the banks and verges of the course, often only inches away from the speeding cars. It was almost inevitable that as car speeds increased – and the faster cars could well be doing 90 to 100 mph or more as they neared the finish – the safety aspect became more worrying as a serious accident was more likely to occur. Such an accident did happen at one of the most popular events in the Home Counties at Kop Hill, near Princes Risborough, Buckingham, in March 1925. This brought an already worrying situation to breaking point and a ban was imposed on the holding of such events on public roads.

Oates' racing Lagonda is joined by a touring stablemate at the Chatcombe Pitch hill-climb in 1921

Let us imagine the scene at a speed hill-climb prior to the ban. Competitors would have been arriving since the early hours, gathering in a makeshift paddock (often literally just that) at the foot of the hill. The bustle and noise in the paddock increases as the roar and crackle of revving engines and open exhausts, the smell of fuel and Castrol 'R' and the haze of exhaust smoke mingles in the warming air as the sun rose to the heat of a summer's day. The practice runs may begin; sometimes there were none, the drivers having to tackle the course virtually unseen unless they happened to be local people who knew it already. Meanwhile the spectators start arriving, on foot, on bicycles and motorbikes, in cars and charabancs. They make their way to precarious vantage points eager to surge forward as favoured cars and drivers make their runs.

The competing cars would usually be run in various classes, by engine capacity, or by definition such as 'Standard Touring Cars', 'Standard Sports Cars', 'Cars of Any Description', 'Amateur' or 'Open', or for Club members only and thus 'Closed'. Occasionally these classes would be further sub-divided by price limits in the standard classes. It would thus be possible for the resourceful driver to run one and the same car in perhaps six different classes, as for example: (i) Standard Sports Cars up to a certain capacity, usually 1100cc or 1500cc; (ii) Cars of any capacity or description; (iii) 'Amateur' class; (iv) 'Open' class; (v) 'Closed' class, and where applicable he could strip off road equipment such as wings, hood, lamps and screen and run the car in the 'Racing' class. The driver would then be eligible for places and awards in any of these classes. Not content with that, some drivers brought more than one car to the event, to run in several different classes, thus further enhancing the chances of success.

As a further variant some clubs devised 'Formula' classes which gave the slower cars some hope of success and helped to even out the disparity of performance between the faster and the slower cars. The Junior Car Club, for example, used the following formula in their Greenhow hill-climb events in 1922 and 1923:

This 1½-litre 'Sascha' Austro-Daimler, an advanced 2-ohc racing *voiturette* of the post-war era, is seen at Sutton Bank in the York & District MCC's speed hill-climb on 28 May 1921. The driver is G.S. Boston who gained a first, second and third place in different classes

$$\frac{\text{Total weight (lbs)}}{\text{time (secs)}^{1.7} \times \text{HP}} \quad \text{where HP was} \atop \text{taken as} \quad \frac{\text{Capacity (cc)}}{\text{100 (Sports classes)} \atop \text{150 (Touring classes)}}$$

Sometimes there was a finishing paddock beyond the finishing line but often, in order to prevent a gathering of competitors' cars beyond this point, cars returned down the hill at the end of each class event. So as the day wore on the spectators had excellent value even if the entry list was comparatively small. In hot or dry weather the cars left a thick dust-cloud in their wake and flying grit and stones showered those nearest to the course. In wet conditions the dust gave way to a shower of muddy water as the cars slid and skidded on the bends. At the close of the day the cars would be driven away from the paddock, the marshals doing their best to sort out the apparent chaos as spectators and their vehicles dispersed . . . and the whole performance would be repeated somewhere else in the country the next weekend until the winter 'dead' season, or the ban.

Above: This 1914 TT Humber racing car seen in the ownership of C. Sgonina at a South Wales event *c.* 1920 exemplifies the kind of performance car that could be bought by enthusiasts after the Great War at a fraction of the cost of any new car of equivalent power. Remarkably, it still survives in very appreciative hands and is regularly raced in vintage events

Below: Little different in conception from racing cars of 1914, this 1918 Straker-Squire is seen at the Spread Eagle hill-climb, near Shaftesbury, in 1922. Its driver was 'Bertie' Kensington Moir, the architect of this novel dazzle-painting. This car also survives today and is still actively used

Above: A 1914 belt-driven GN cycle-car is seen here at an early post-war speed hill-climb at Style Cop, Staffordshire, in 1919

Inset: Bliss in a GN. H. Bliss's car, registered U 9338 and finished in red tackles Greenhow hill-climb on 22 July 1922

The GN was one of the most popular sporting cycle-cars. Here is Capt Trubie Moore at the Harrogate & District MCC's speed hill-climb on 28 May 1921

Who better to demonstrate the GN's abilities than Capt 'Archie' Frazer-Nash, the 'N' of 'GN', in *Kim* at Sutton Bank, Yorkshire, in 1919? The single oil-lamp paid lip service to legality when the car was driven to and from events

Seen in the 'paddock', Capt Arthur Waite's sporting Austin Twenty simmers in the sunshine between runs at the same event. Motor cycles formed the bulk of the entry and some of them can be seen here

Quite sober motor cars were entered for speed events even though their top speed had no hope of matching that of much faster rivals. To even the balance these touring cars were entered in the 'Formula' classes, run on a formula devised by the promoting club. Here a 10/20 Bayliss Thomas in full touring trim climbs Angel Bank, Shropshire, on 23 September 1922

Inset: G.S. Boston's Austro-Daimler stripped only of wings is seen 100 yd or so farther up the hill at Angel Bank on 21 April 1923. His was one of the faster climbs of this SUNBAC event.

An essential preliminary to these events was the weighing of the competing cars or motor cycles at a local weighbridge, often at the nearest railway station. On the weighbridge prior to a speed hill-climb at Greenhow Hill, near Pately Bridge, on 22 July 1922 is Harry Hodgson's 11.9 hp Hodgson Super-Sports, still waiting for its competition number (3) to be painted on. E.R. Hall's Bugatti and A.K. Dawson's Hillman await their turn

A Mathis tackles the stones and gulleys of the 'freak' hill-climb at Rosedale Abbey Bank, Yorkshire, of which a local paper wrote proudly: 'There is hardly a severer climbing test in the whole of England'

One of the 1921 200-Miles Race team of GNs, still showing traces of its race number 2 on that occasion, is seen here at Staxton hill-climb, near Scarborough, on 27 April 1922 with Capt. Trubie Moore at the wheel

E.R. Hall, a staunch Yorkshireman as well as a skilled and versatile driver, is seen here at Aston Clinton, near Tring. His car is the famous Aston Martin *Bunny*, here with 2-ohc engine. Hall corrects a skid as he puts up a fast time on 16 September 1922

N.T. Beardsell's Hodgson takes a dashing line through the sharp bend at Greenhow hill-climb on 23 June 1923, throwing up a fine dust-cloud. His best time was 1 min 36.2 sec for the measured mile

Irrepressible as ever, E.R. Hall fielded two cars for this event which was organized by the Yorkshire centre of the Junior Car Club. Here he corners his 8/18 Talbot with much verve to record 1 min 46 sec on this first real summer day of the 1923 season. His other entry was a Bugatti

The 2.30 p.m. start of the 1923 Greenhow climb was delayed by the passage of cows on the hill. They took an almost unbelievable 52 min to clear the finishing line, after which the faster stuff could have a go

Below: Greenhow again. The sun shines warmly and even the marshals do not seem unduly put out by the bovine delay as they prepare to board their transport up the hill

Capt Trubie Moore (leaning on car) was a regular and very successful driver in northern events with his GN and Horstman. Both cars are seen here at Greenhow on 23 June 1923

E.R. Hall's Bugatti enjoys a peaceful interlude between runs at the York & District MCC's speed hill-climb at Garrowby, near Stamford Bridge, on 26 August 1922. The course was approximately 1 km in length

Cyril Paul's Beardmore was often 'in the money' at speed events in the early 1920s. He is seen here at the South Wales AC's Caerphilly hill-climb on 29 June 1923. As can be seen from the crowds this was a most popular event

Competitors and spectators at Garrowby on 20 June 1923 could refresh themselves at this Ford-T fish-and-chip van parked among the cow parsley on the verge. One applauds the photographer for including this human touch

Capt G.E.T. Eyston, later to become famous as a record breaker, is seen here with his 2-ohc Aston Martin at South Harting on the scarp slope of the South Downs on 28 July 1923

More refreshments . . . and Capt Trubie Moore's GN (now entered as a Frazer Nash) and his Horstman stand side by side in the paddock at Sutton Bank on 26 April 1924. Moore also entered a 10.8 hp Darracq in this event. The small boy beside the Horstman is Moore's son, Geoffrey

A rare bird indeed. J.P. Prior drives W. Hallett's Marlborough at Holme Moss hill-climb, September 1924. He seems happy at the prospect

Already a name to be conjured with, a youthful Raymond Mays is seen here at the wheel of his Bugatti with which he put up a time of 77.2 sec over the 1¼-mile course after a spectacular climb, only to crash after crossing the finishing line

Kop Hill, near Princes Risborough, was a popular favourite. The course of 902 yd led up the scarp slope of the Chilterns. Here A.G. Gripper takes his 3-litre Bentley up the hill between the densely packed spectators who line the verges to within inches of the passing cars. After a serious accident on this hill in March 1925, a ban on such events was imposed

Miss M. Mitchell at the wheel of the 24/90 Straker-Squire she drove at Holme Moss, September 1924. Some female spectators take a keen interest

SPEED TRIALS

Speed trials on the level, as opposed to speed hill-climbs, were another very popular outlet for the sporting enthusiast of the 1920s. Sometimes these were held on suitable stretches of public road (with the cooperation of the local police authorities), but more popular still were the promenades of seaside towns, such as Herne Bay in Kent. Here in June 1924 the legendary Count Louis Zborowski entered his splendid Hispano-Suiza in the touring class for cars over 1500cc, and his fast and dangerous Mercedes in the racing class. This was the car in which he was so tragically killed at Monza only three months later.

Some of these promenades, such as those at Southsea and Blackpool, were wide enough to enable the cars to race in pairs which made for much greater spectator appeal than did the sight of a single car, no matter how fast, running up the course on its own. At the Blackpool Speed Trials of 1923, for example, there were some 130 motor cycle entries and nearly 80 cars, the entire field being divided into no fewer than thirty-two classes. Cars and motor cycles ran separately, but in both cases they ran in pairs over the 1 km course along Queens Drive. The event occupied seven hours and was attended by many thousands of spectators.

Events of this importance attracted many of the big names. In 1924 the Blackpool entry list included those of J.A. Joyce (A.C.), L. Cushman (Bugatti), Capt J.E.P. Howey (Leyland Eight), R. Mays (Bugatti), Malcolm Campbell (8-cyl Ballot) (he had driven his 350 hp V-12 Sunbeam land speed record car and his 17 hp Itala in the 1923 event), Dario Resta (Sunbeam), B.H. Davenport (GN), Cyril Paul (Beardmore) and the as yet relatively unknown H.R.S. Birkin (later Sir Henry of Bentley fame) who on this occasion drove

Spectators seem scanty at this rather bleak-looking but unidentified speed trial at which a sports Morris Cowley speeds towards the camera

the Birkin-Comery, a 2-litre car with an engine designed by W.S. Comery and financed by Birkin, on an Aston Martin chassis.

At the contrasting end of the scale some such speed events were held on private roads such as the dead straight Gloucester Drive on Earl Beauchamp's estate at Madresfield, near Malvern. This attractive setting with its wide grass verges and park-like trees that were in their infancy in the early 1920s is still used by the Vintage Sports Car Club, keeping up a tradition of motor speed events that dates back to before World War I.

Speed trials on the level demanded a good power-to-weight ratio and rapid acceleration, but did not necessarily require the standards of braking and road-holding essential for a speed hill-climb with its combination of bends and gradients. It was seldom easy, however, to find a suitable stretch of straight, level road that would provide a really long course, since there had to be enough room beyond the finishing line for the fastest cars to pull up safely. It was the search for longer, level courses that had turned the attention of the promoting clubs to the wide expanses of sandy sea-shore that abound round Britain's coasts, but sand racing is so specialized an art that it deserves attention in its own right.

Sporting versions of the Morris Cowley and Hillman are seen here approaching the start line for a sprint, possibly organized by the Cambridge University Automobile Club, *c.* 1921

Cycle-cars to the fore in the form of a GN, Morgan and, on the right, two AVs await their turn for starter's orders at the Liverpool Motor Club's Storeton Speed Trials in 1920. This was a flat course of 1,093 yd

Heavier metal at the same event. Nearest the camera is the early 30/98 Vauxhall driven by W. Watson who had driven the winning Hutton in the 1908 'Four Inch' TT and also drove Vauxhalls in pre-World War I races. Behind the Vauxhall is one of the 1914 TT Sunbeams, driven here by L.V. Cozens. It seems to be the centre of attraction

Capt Trubie Moore glances, smiling, backwards as he prepares to take his Horstman which to quote a press report,'roared down the track at 96 miles an hour', at the Morecambe Open Speed Trials on 17 September 1923. This shot displays the car's elegant lines well

Miss Mitchell's Straker-Squire seen at speed on 6 September 1924 at the York & District MC's Knavesmire Speed Trials, York

Moore's Horstman (No. 7) and his GN being prepared for their runs at a northern speed event, c. 1922. Also in the picture is a Rhode (NW 811) and part of an HE

The Super-Sports Horstman succeeded better than most in marrying a narrow, angular radiator shape to the smooth, bulbous lines of the sporting body. Here Moore's Horstman is on the line, poised for the 'off'

Raymond Mays' famous Bugatti *Cordon Rouge* receives attention from Amherst Villiers at the Madresfield Speed Trials on 22 June 1922. Mays gained ftd on this occasion as he did on so many others

This Horstman is that of G.S. Boston, seen on the start line for the Blackpool Speed Trials, 16 June 1923. Also visible are the Crouch (No. 159) of A.E. Moss and the Horstman (No. 149) of Trubie Moore

The ubiquitous Moore *equipe* seen at the York & District MC's Knavesmire Speed Trials on 5 September 1925. This was a sprint over approximately ⅓-mile on a concrete road. The cars are (left to right) 11.9 hp Horstman, 8.7 hp Frazer Nash *Akela* and 11.9 hp Frazer Nash. Moore's times with these cars were 24.2 sec, 22.4 sec and 27.8 sec respectively

A famous car in new ownership. This is one of the 2-ohc Aston Martins raced by Count 'Lou' Zborowski in 1922/3. After his death at Monza in October 1924, it changed hands and is seen, still in Zborowski's white finish, driven by a Mr Pearson of Sutton Coldfield at a speed trial near Stalybridge

Above: An animated scene at a northern speed event where a Salmson awaits the action on 30 April 1927

Top left: Capt C.M. Harvey's Alvis is seen here between runs at the Morecambe Speed Trials, 17 September 1923. These were held on the Lancaster to Morecambe New Road over a 1 km course

Bottom left: The Rhode was a Birmingham-built small car which, though not manufactured in large numbers, always had sporting pretensions. This 10.8 hp model had a push-rod ohv engine, smoother than its predecessors but not very fast. Capt C. Gray, of the Rhode Motor Co. is at the wheel, competing at the Knavesmire Speed Trials, York

SAND RACING

Almost from the earliest days of motoring those with speed in mind sought the wide open spaces of the extensive sandy beaches around the coasts of Britain as excellent places at which to indulge in unrestricted speed. Some of these sites were remote but those nearer to existing seaside resorts became another attraction for tourists who came in larger numbers still when speed events were held. Crowds of over 15,000 attended many of the Southport sand races, for example.

Pendine, Porthcawl, Saltburn, Skegness and South- port and Weston-super-Mare spring readily to mind as popular locations for this specialized form of motor racing. With the tide out such beaches exposed miles of sand, making it easy to provide a course of suitable length for even the fastest cars. Competitors in the flying start events at Saltburn could take a run of 2½ miles before entering the measured distance and still leave room after the finishing line to pull up safely. Indeed, most of the land speed record attempts of the decade were carried out on such beaches.

Even so it was not all plain sailing. The sand surface could vary from dry through clogging to waterlogged, and was seldom really smooth. Always the sea was moving in to trap the unwary on the incoming tide. Often the closing stages of sand events would see competitors snaking away over a narrowing strip of sand that was already awash with sea water. 'With neither modesty nor consideration, the gentle waves of the North Sea were all but lapping the course as the final event was run off' commented *The Light Car & Cycle car* of a 1924 event at Skegness. The cars would be almost lost in flying sand grains and clouds of spume, and the drivers' visibility would be cut to the minimum.

In races of many laps, which were possible where the area of sand was wide enough to allow turning markers, the corners would become badly churned up by each successive car, making it increasingly hard to pick a smooth path without serious loss of time or even of control. It was at Southport that May Cunliffe had the misfortune to become 'tramlined' in these ruts with her supercharged GP Sunbeam, which rolled over several times, resulting in the death of her father who was acting as riding mechanic.

The combination of flying sand grains, salt water and a salty atmosphere was extremely tough on machinery, particularly in the more sensitive parts of engines and superchargers. Despite these hazards the popularity of sand racing was boosted by the 1925 ban on speed events on public roads. Venues such as Southport, Pendine and Skegness continued to host sand events right through and beyond the 1920s.

It is perhaps strange that among the sand racing car drivers no one name comes readily to mind as that of a driver whose reputation was made solely on sand. Many of the famous took part but all achieved greater fame for their racing skills and successes in different environments.

Above: The sands at Porthcawl were more popular for club events as they were less remote than other venues. The South Wales AC regularly staged what became known as 'The Welsh Double', a two-day event consisting of a speed hill-climb at Caerphilly and speed trials on Porthcawl sands. Here Capt G.E.T. Eyston moves the gear lever into second as he accelerates away over the wet sands in his 2-ohc Aston Martin

Top left: T. Gilmore-Ellis drove this GN, which displays its characteristic off-side starting-handle, at the Weston Speed Trials on 30 August 1919. The side starting-handle was often the butt of small boys who would gleefully shout 'Mind yer don't bust the elastic!'

Bottom left: The sands of Pendine, South Wales, achieved fame as the setting for many a land speed record. They were also used for club events and here we see Cardiff man C. Sgonina with his GN with which he took a first place at the Carmarthen & District MC's 1922 event

As a make, the Beardmore is chiefly remembered for its taxi-cabs, but in the 1920s the firm backed a very successful sporting programme. Cyril Paul, seen here as he speeds past a solitary official at Scarborough, was by far the firm's best driver

A famous car in unpractised hands is the ex-Mays Bugatti *Cordon Bleu*, seen here being driven by Francis Giveen at a Southport sands meeting in 1925. This car with the same driver had such a nasty moment at Kop Hill in March 1925 that the meeting was abandoned and a ban placed on speed trials on public roads

A.C. Cars Ltd of Thames Ditton, Surrey had a formidable publicist in the form of S.F. Edge. They also had a driver of great skill – J.A. Joyce, whose single-seater model seen here receives attention at a Southport meeting in September 1925

R.T. Horton's Morgan (No. 67) partially obscures E.A. Mayner's white Targa Florio Mercedes in this busy Southport scene in September 1925. Horton later achieved much success at Brooklands events and elsewhere with special versions of the M.G. Midget and Magnette. The Mercedes survives today in appreciative ownership

Tails! No. 32 is the unique SR (Spurrier-Railton) pre-prototype for the Arab sports car with Railton's modified version of Parry Thomas' single-ohc engine. It is driven here by Kenneth Parker. Alongside is G.H. Taylor's Alvis (No. 65) at Southport in 1925

Broadside view of Taylor's Alvis, again at Southport in 1925. This is a type SA 12/40; its present whereabouts is unknown, but it was at one time owned by the editor of *Motor Sport*, Bill Boddy

H.F. Clay's elderly but fast 1914 TT Vauxhall is set against a typical backdrop of sea and sand at Southport, 1925

To the left is the clearly recognizable form of a GP Bugatti but on the right is a rare supercharged Arab driven by Henry (later Sir Henry) Spurrier of Leyland. The scene is Southport, so convenient to Leyland, and the date is *c.* 1926

Kaye Don's Sunbeam *The Cub* seen in repose at a Southport event *c.* 1929. The shrouded radiator and the gloomy faces might suggest that something is amiss on this occasion

Southport events attracted big names and here we see H.O.D. Segrave's GP Sunbeam surrounded by interested hero-worshippers. Dashing and debonair, his cars always as immaculately turned out as he was, Segrave became the first man to be knighted for a World Land Speed Record success for Britain in 1929

Poised for the drop of the starter's flag at this Southport meeting are G.L. Jones (Bugatti) and Byrom (Austin Seven)

Above: Huge crowds line the sands as a Gordon England Austin Seven with Percy Stephenson at the wheel spurts sand from its wheels at a Southport meeting, *c.* 1929

Below: Determined small fry in the shape of (left to right) B. Thompson's Triumph Super Seven and the Austins of Stephenson and Byrom grace this shot at Southport, *c.* 1929

Another of the legendary figures of motor racing was Malcolm Campbell, whose beautiful sleek Delage is the focus of much interest at a later Southport meeting

SHELSLEY WALSH

This speed hill-climb situated in the quiet beauty of Worcestershire among the orchards and hop-yards of the Teme valley has become world-famous wherever motor racing enthusiasts gather. The Midland Automobile Club had held such climbs on other sites on public roads from its inception early this century. The Club settled on this private road that snakes invitingly away from the orchards of the valley towards the steepening wooded slopes that top the skyline in 1905, so that this is now by far the oldest site in the country to be used for hill-climbing at speed.

For many years, certainly throughout and beyond the 1920s, the paddock and start area had all the atmosphere of the farmyard that it was. Relatively little has changed today so that it is easy for anyone familiar with the hill over many years to absorb Shelsley's unique atmosphere. During and after the 1920s a special 'Amateur' event was held in addition to the 'Open' events at other times of the year and many a driver later destined for fame first competed in these well-supported 'Amateur' climbs. As the course was on a private road its importance received a welcome boost when numerous speed hill-climbs held on public roads all over the country suffered an embargo in March 1925, so that by 1930 Shelsley Walsh had achieved international status. It would be invidious to single out the cars and drivers that epitomized Shelsley in the 1920s, but perhaps the names of Raymond Mays with his Bugattis and the Vauxhall-Villiers and of Basil Davenport with his GN *Spider* must be regarded as the legends of the decade and, happily, later.

Shelsley could certainly be wet. On many occasions the rain fell relentlessly, turning the course into a river of red marl and rusty-looking water up which

Few aces of the Grand Prix circuits did well at Shelsley. Here H.O.D. Segrave takes his Sunbeam up the hill to record 53.8 sec in 1925. Although it was ftd it was not a record. However, such names were splendid crowd pullers

the cars would slither and slide, showering one and all with a russet spray. The rain would turn the banks into slippery mud slides on which spectators and officials could barely keep their feet. Whatever its moods Shelsley cast its spell on competitors and spectators alike. Few other speed events have ever rivalled the friendly, close-knit atmosphere of a very special family thoroughly enjoying themselves that was the hallmark of this famous event.

Raymond Mays brings the Vauxhall-Villiers back down the hill after gaining ftd and a new record at 45.6 sec at the September 1929 event. Note his pioneering use of twin rear wheels. Peter Berthon is in the passenger's seat

A luxury car lets its hair down. G. Summers' Silver Ghost Rolls-Royce hugs the corner closely at the bottom 'Esses' in this 1922 climb. The spectators are unnervingly close to the inside of the bend

This view of the Shelsley car park provides a magnificent display of vehicles upon which to test one's powers of recognition. This picture dates from *c.* 1922

Count Louis Zborowski with the countess beside him are seen in a brand new 2-ohc Aston Martin in 1922 at his home at Higham in Kent. The bonnet straps and wire gauze screen for the driver have yet to be fitted

Above: Noel Beardsell's Hodgson seen
before the hair-raising evolutions in
which he indulged in a spirited run at
the July 1924 meeting. The car ended its
run broadside-on across a 4 ft-deep
ditch

Inset: The camera has captured Clay's
3-litre Bentley making the first climb of
Shelsley by this make in 1922. His time
was 66.8 sec

Eddie Hall, one of the most consistent performers over the years at Shelsley with a wide variety of cars, reaches for the handbrake as he crosses the finishing line in his Bugatti at the September 1922 meeting. His time was 60.8 sec

Cyril Paul, a most versatile driver, enjoyed many successes with the racing Beardmores but few could have pleased him more than his ftd at the 1924 meeting

R.F. Summers clips the lower S-bend closely in his sports Aston Martin in the July 1924 meeting, while his passenger tries to emulate the antics of racing sidecar passengers

The 3-litre 2-ohc Vauxhalls designed for the 1922 TT were debarred by their engine capacity from Grand Prix events on account of the changed formula. For Brooklands and British sprints and hill-climbs such restrictions did not apply and here we see Humphrey Cook's car at the September 1923 meeting. Note the characteristic large diameter six-spoke steering-wheel

Summers again, this time with the 30/98 Vauxhall and some more acrobatic passengers in the 1925 event. Spectators had now been banned from crowding the inside of the corner (*vide* notice) but even so one miscreant crouches among the bushes

Were it not for the crowds, the press and the officials, there would be little to suggest a speed hill-climb as this 10/20 Bayliss Thomas, sedate and fully laden, climbs Shelsley in 1922

Above: The Alvis Car & Engineering Co. Ltd actively supported a racing programme. Surprisingly, they abandoned orthodoxy and turned out a technically advanced front-wheel drive racing car in 1925. Its handling took a bit of getting used to, and here we can see C.M. Harvey in one of the fwd racers approaching the 'Esses' in 1925. The car was nicknamed 'Tadpole'

Inset: Raymond Mays first competed at Shelsley in 1921 with a Hillman 10 hp, and subsequently in his Bugattis, but here, in 1925, he pins his faith on a special A.C. Unfortunately this was one of his rare off days

Above: Alvis sports cars were, by contrast, quite orthodox, which made them popular and successful. A.G. Gripper's 12/50 model, seen here on the lower slopes of the hill in 1926, was widely used in competition as well as being used as an ordinary road car

Inset: Cyril Paul, no stranger to the hill, brings his 2-litre GP Sunbeam through the dappled sunlight on 4 September 1926 to record 50.6 sec, not good enough to beat B.H. Davenport or Raymond Mays on this occasion

Miss May Cunliffe, always a spirited driver, about to leave the line with her 3-litre Bentley, one of the 1922 TT team cars, at the September 1926 meeting. Weather conditions had caused the July meeting to be postponed that year in which she would normally have taken part

The July amateur meetings were about as well attended as the Open meeting in September. Here a Frazer Nash enters the 'Esses' in this pleasing view of the 1927 Amateur meeting

Above: Lost in the countryside? No, this is the finishing paddock at the top of the hill and Dudley Jevons' straight-eight Bugatti is being admired by a cloche-hatted lady at the meeting of 5 May 1928

Below: This shot of the paddock taken at the 1927 Amateur meeting could easily be mistaken for a picture of a well attended farm sale were it not for the competition number seen beside Harry Reigate's 3-litre Invicta

Cyril Paul again demonstrates his versatility as he takes his 15/60 Alfa Romeo up the hill in the Formula class at the July 1928 Amateur meeting. He recorded 81.8 sec with this well-laden car

Heavy metal. Earl Howe's ex-Caracciola 38/250 TT Mercedes Benz fresh from its TT win reposes in the paddock. Howe's times were 48.0 sec and 47.6 sec on his two runs at this September 1929 meeting

TOURIST TROPHY

Although the Tourist Trophy Races only impinged on the opening and closing years of the decade, their importance and influence justify their inclusion here in a category of their own.

The Isle of Man staged the first TT in 1905 and the event was run again in 1906, 1907 and 1908. The regulations for those early years were far from uniform and by 1908, the year of the famous 'Four-Inch' race (so named because a 4-in cylinder bore was the maximum permitted), the cars had no real resemblance to touring vehicles. They were less so in 1914, the next year in which the race was held, for by that year the cars had become out and out racing machines.

In 1922 the Isle of Man hosted its last Tourist Trophy, the cars once again being true racers. In that year the event was really a race within a race as a 1500 Trophy was run concurrently for cars below that engine capacity. In the main event won, as in 1914, by Sunbeam the maximum engine capacity was 3- litres.

The appeal of a road race for 'touring' machines i.e., cars with full road equipment, was strong and moves were made to reinstate the race in Ulster on the Ards circuit south of Belfast. An Irish location was chosen because mainland Britain, always having taken a less enlightened view than the Manx and Irish authorities, would not allow racing on public roads.

On 18 August 1928 the first of the new series of Tourist Trophy races was run on that new but very demanding circuit. It proved to be a great success and the same circuit was used annually without a break until an unfortunate accident in the 1936 event led to the decision to discontinue the race on the Ards circuit.

The 1928 race was so successful that in the following year the event had sufficient cachet to attract the big Bentleys, the Mercedes Benz team, the Bugattis and Alfa-Romeos that were so prominent at Le Mans, and famous continental drivers were keen to enter. The Tourist Trophy had really 'arrived' and the soubriquet 'TT' became an even more potent word in the language of motor sport enthusiasts than it had been in the early days on Manx soil.

Run concurrently with the 3-litre race was a 1500cc class. Lionel Martin had hoped to field his new 2-ohc racers but they were not ready in time so the famous old-stager *Bunny* with sv engine was the sole Aston Martin contender in Kensington Moir's hands. He retired with valve trouble

The Isle of Man, traditional home of the Tourist Trophy, hosted its last TT races on 22 June 1922. W.O. Bentley's 3-litre cars, a make new to the post-war sporting scene, were represented by a team of three. In appalling weather conditions they did well to finish in second, fourth and fifth places, driven by Clement, W.O. Bentley himself and W.D. Hawkes. Here 'W.O.' corners in the wet, barely protected by the o/s front mudguard rigged for the occasion. Bentley won the team award for this performance

Victory in the 1922 event went to Sunbeam in the hands of Chassagne. Segrave's car is seen here. He put up the fastest lap before retiring

Vauxhalls had been cruelly disappointed in the 1914 TT, so for 1922 H.R. Ricardo designed a very advanced new 2-ohc engine for their TT entries. A team of three entered but a third place was the best they could do. Here Payne's car rounds Governor's Bridge in one of the few moments of the race when rain was not actually falling

Victory in the 1500cc race went, as expected, to the Talbot-Darracq stable. They took first and second places. Here the winner, Algy Lee Guinness (with hand on bonnet) stands with the victorious car. Beside him stand Coatalen, the designer (in Homburg hat) and an immaculate Henry Segrave

Above: The 1929 fwd Alvis team for the TT is seen here. From left to right the cars are those of C.M. Harvey, L. Cushman and Cyril Paul. They finished tenth, eighth and seventeenth respectively.

Above left: The Tourist Trophy was revived in Ireland for 1928, since the British mainland would not countenance racing on a public road circuit. Two of the fwd Alvis team, W. Urquhart Dykes (No. 23) and L. Cushman (No. 32) are seen here on the Ards circuit on 18 August 1928. To aid pitwork and recognition on the course the Alvis cars carried the initial letter of their driver's surname on the nearside headlamp. Dykes crashed after 15 laps but Cushman finished a very creditable second overall, only 13 sec behind the winning Lea-Francis of Kaye Don.

Below left: The 1929 race was held on 17 August and the success of the previous year's race attracted a field of seventy-three cars. Here is a splendid action shot of Otto Merz in his 7,100cc supercharged Mercedes Benz travelling at 110 mph. Alas, he was disqualified for removing a damaged wing even though he had finished but he had the satisfaction of seeing his team mate Rudi Caracciola come home a most deserving winner

ROAD TRIALS

The Road Trial is perhaps the basic form of motor sport in that 'in essence' it involves no more than travelling by car from A to B, as did the Paris–Rouen Trial of 1894. The 'sport' lies in the challenges imposed by the route, any tests that may be incorporated along that route, and the challenge of one's rivals in the same event.

As cars became more reliable so the road trials became more severe as the capabilities of cars and drivers were tested in harder conditions. Even before 1914 many of the classic trials that survived throughout the 1920s had already attracted a following. Also minor road trials promoted by various motor clubs up and down the country were widespread almost every weekend of the year.

The toughest road trials took place in the winter quarter of the year when the weather might be expected to throw in a few additional hazards for cars and drivers. The major long-distance events that became annual fixtures in the motor sporting calendar, such as the London–Exeter, held in late December, the London–Land's End held at Easter and the London–Edinburgh held at Whitsun attracted huge entry lists. There was also the Land's End–John O'Groats Trial, a two-day marathon held in mid-summer to take advantage of the northern daylight hours and which covered 875 miles, while the Six-Days Trials, as their name implies, were of even longer duration and mileage.

One must bear in mind that in the 1920s most competing cars were open tourers or sports models with scanty, if any, weather protection and were far removed from the comfort and ease of modern motoring. Most cars ran on narrow, high-pressure beaded-edge tyres, many had only rear-wheel

T.A.N. Leadbetter's Alvis takes to the narrows in this section of the £1,000 Trial of 7 July 1925

brakes, and electrical systems and windscreen wipers were nowhere near as reliable and efficient as they are today. Above all, perhaps, was the fact that road surfaces were universally much inferior to those of today. On the rural tracks and lanes and gradients so beloved of the trials organizers road 'surfaces' could only be described as diabolical. This was particularly so in the very areas that the toughest and longest of these road trials invariably covered such as Scotland, the Lake District, the Pennines, the Cotswolds, the West Country and Wales.

Yet almost every weekend of the year the regular competitors were out on different trials across the country. Many of these entries were 'Trade' — motor manufacturers or their representatives, agents and retailers. An attempt was made in the mid-1920s to bar trade entries but this so decimated the entry lists that it was totally unsatisfactory and the ban was shortlived. Manufacturers saw their cars' performances in these trials as a valuable advertising and indeed this was the case. However, the same 'Trade' interests were not always so open in disclosing some of the tricks of the trade that led to success. Nevertheless, these events retained their popularity in the eyes of the public because the cars were recognizably akin to the cars they could buy for themselves. By the end of the decade the performance of the average car had improved almost out of recognition due, largely, to the lessons of such events.

A Morris Cowley — unusually the Traveller's Brougham model — is seen taking part in the £1,000 Trial on 7 July 1925. This event took in much of the difficult Pennine country without resorting to any freakish sections

This Bayliss Thomas on trade plates was awarded the Club Tankard for its performance in the Midland Car Club's Trial of 21 October 1922

A.G. Gripper takes his 2-litre H.E. through the tribulations of the London–Holyhead Trial, 1922, the particular tribulation in this case being the notorious Bwlch-y-Groes in Wales. He is followed by a Gwynne and an Angus-Sanderson

The majority of road trials in the 1920s catered for motor cycles as well as cars, the two-wheelers often forming the greater part of the entry. Here the driver of a 9.8 hp Rhode and a motor cycle competitor pose for the camera at a northern trial, 1922

A Morgan squeezes past an earlier form of transport while climbing Lynmouth Hill on the 1923 London–Land's End Trial. Although it had many aspiring rivals the Morgan was unquestionably the most successful British three-wheeler of the 1920s

Inset: Bare hedges and early spring sunshine give light and shade to this sports model Bayliss Thomas competing in the Midland Car Club's Trial of 3 March 1923

Below: A favourite spot for spectators and camera-men was the hairpin on Blue Hills Mine which had to be tackled by competitors in the annual London– Land's End Trials of the MCC. Here A.R. Abbott's air-cooled Rover Eight found no problems in 1924, the first year this hill was included

Inset: In the £1,000 Trial, held on 7 July 1925, A.R. Abbott's Clyno leads a Crossley saloon on a moorland road. At one time Clyno were serious rivals to Morris as a popular touring car, but by 1929 the firm was in decline, finally ceasing production all together the following year

Below: Three-wheelers like the popular and very successful Morgan were eligible for both car and motor cycle events. That the going could be very rough indeed may be seen in this shot of an Aero Morgan and sundry motor-cyclists competing in the Scottish Six-Days Trial

The major long-distance trials such as the London–Edinburgh were well-established and attracted big entry lists, as may be seen from the competition numbers displayed. Here a d'Yrsan three-wheeler is sandwiched between two Clynos in the 1925 event, while somebody's house move is captured for posterity

Inset: Tough, fast and versatile might fairly sum up the attributes of the Alvis 12/50. As a make, Alvis commanded a very loyal following. Here A.G. Gripper takes his much-used sports model trialling in 1926

Below: G.H. Goodall with N.W. Slatter as navigator are seen on a sunny day in 1926 tackling the International Six-Days Trial with their Aero Morgan

Above: Always a favoured vantage point, even to the extent of climbing trees to obtain a better view, Beggars Roost was included in many of the well-known trials to the West Country. Here an A.B.C. has succumbed to the gradient in the London–Land's End Trial, 1927

Below left: This stolid 14 hp Armstrong Siddeley saloon has managed to keep going, certainly in bottom gear, avoiding the attentions of the rope party in the same event

Below right: Alas, this Alvis tourer has lost any chance of a gold medal, though perhaps the stalwarts on the rope deserve one

A line of Invictas and one 14/60 Lagonda semi-sports tourer bringing up the rear in the London–Edinburgh Trial of 1928. The Invicta drivers were Ahern (No. 269) Leapman (No. 271) and Reigate (No. 270)

Drawn up at another Yorkshire meet in 1922 are (left to right) Essex, Hurtu, Palladium, Horstman, Jowett, GN, Jowett and Singer

A Rolls-Royce Phantom I fabric-bodied saloon makes its luxurious way northwards in the same event, followed by J. Ahern's 3-litre Invicta tourer

A Delage saloon driven by A.G. Gripper squeezes past a failed Morris Oxford saloon in the 1928 London–Edinburgh Trial

Blue Hills Mine again, this time in 1929. Protective railings have now appeared (compare with picture on p. 93) and the car is A.G. Gripper's fwd Alvis sports model in the London–Land's End Trial

MOTOR CYCLING

It may be said, perhaps with some truth, that the two-wheel motoring enthusiasts have always been more sportingly inclined, as a body, than their four-wheel counterparts. If one took a random selection of motorists as compared with motor-cyclists a higher percentage of the latter would take an interest in or practise the sporting side of motoring. Certainly it is true that one could buy and run a sporting motor cycle that would out-perform most cars on the road, whatever the performance pretensions of the cars, for a fraction of the cost that would be incurred in order to obtain anything like the equivalent on four wheels.

The sports car of the 1920s may indeed have made few concessions to comfort or to our fickle and often inclement weather. The sporting motor-cyclist, however, had to forego even those spartan comforts, relying as he did solely on the protection afforded to him by his leathers and sidcot. To him these were trifling considerations when weighed against the elemental joys of the road which the hearty performance of his machine could give. In those far-off days one could legally drive any motor cycle at the tender age of fourteen, and a true tale is told of one such lad, later to become well-known, who rode a very 'hot' Norton to five 'firsts' in a speed hill-climb on the day of his fourteenth birthday.

The sporting motor-cyclist of the 1920s had all the choices of sprints, hill-climbs, sand-racing, Brooklands races and road trials that were available to the sporting motorist. At many such events motor cycles outnumbered cars. For many sporting motor-cyclists there was one supreme event in the calendar, the Tourist Trophy races in the Isle of Man, races that had formed an unbroken series (apart from the years

An unknown competitor returns past the finishing line at the Worcester & District MCC's event at Madresfield Court in 1921

1915–1919) since their inception in 1907, two years after the first of the TTs for cars.

A reminiscence from Charlie Sgonina, the Welshman famed for his motor cycling prowess, is worth quoting: 'The next event was the 500-Miles Race at Brooklands [the 1921 race] and as I had never been on the track before it was quite an experience and great fun. Freddie Dixon burst a tyre in front of me and was thrown at about 90 mph. He rolled over and over, bits of his clothing coming off, and I thought, "Poor old Freddie won't be riding again for a long time", but he was really tough and I noticed him later on back in the race again.' Freddie was indeed tougher than most and made a great name for himself as a motorcyclist long before he became almost as legendary a figure on four wheels. Not all could equal his toughness or his skill but the story well illustrates the spirit of the sporting motor-cyclist of the time for whom his machine and his sport were a way of life.

The Tourist Trophy Races in the Isle of Man were a major draw in the annual sporting calendar. Here we see Eric Williams bringing his winning A.J.S. round the 'Gooseneck' in the 1921 Junior TT

Getting there. One way to get the bike to the event was to lash it on the running-board of a car. Here a Cubitt car is used to transport a competing Excelsior motor cycle, *c.* 1922. By strange coincidence the great George Dance used a Cubitt car to transport his sprint Sunbeam in a similar fashion

An unknown competitor, head down and cap flat-a-back, speeds up Chatcombe Pitch hill-climb, near Cheltenham, in 1921. The course was approximately half a mile in length, rising up the Cotswold scarp

Inset: Hero worship. George Dance himself with his sprint Sunbeam at the Weston Speed Trials, 1919. He seems to be keenly watching the progress of a rival competitor away in the distance – the locals watch him

Below: Competitors at Orton Scar hill-climb, 1919. 'Pa' Cowley is the bearded figure on the left, G.S. Boston is in the centre and Caldwell on the right. Boston looks nonchalant, the others purposeful

Crouched as low as possible, George Dance speeds past the eager spectators at the Storeton Open Speed Trials, 15 May 1920

The sidecar class line up for the start of one of their events at Brooklands on 29 May 1920. F. Barnes is seen in conversation with T.W. Loughborough, Secretary of the ACU (centre)

Above: Brooklands track re-opened after the First World War in 1920, much to the delight of the motor cycle racing fraternity who were glad to get back into competition. Competitors in the 500cc class line up for the start on 29 May 1920. On the left is Mrs Eric Longden, standing beside Emmerson's A.B.C. which she rode to victory

Inset: G.S. Boston's A.J.S. sidecar outfit at the same event. He came home with a first and a second place awards

The ever active Boston is seen here with his A.J.S. on the start line for the Sutton Bank hill-climb on 21 August 1920. The gathered officials and spectators are worth studying

Machine and rider crest the ridge at the Newcastle hill-climb at Muggleswick Common on 30 July 1921 . . . and it's Boston with his A.J.S. again. He certainly got around

Above: H.R. Davies is seen here astride his racing A.J.S. combination at the foot of the Test Hill at Brooklands on 20 October 1920. After his A.J.S. days he went into manufacture with the H.R.D. machines

Top right: F.W. ('Freddie') Dixon with his Harley-Davidson outfit at Sutton Bank on 16 April 1921. He put up ftd so no wonder he's smiling

Bottom right: The 1921 A.J.S. team for the Junior TT is seen here with (left to right) R.F. Harris, H.R. Davies and Eric Williams. Howard Davies made TT history by riding his 'Junior' A.J.S. to win the Senior race as well

Here the Triumph team for the 1921 Senior TT is lined up prior to the race. Left to right are C. Sgonina, S. Gill, G.J. Sheman and H. Pattinson, the latter a private entrant

It's that man again. Boston's A.J.S. outfit on the line at the Angel Bank hill-climb on 23 September 1922, where he gained two 'firsts'. Vic Horsman stands on the extreme left

Typical of the keen amateur, this is G. Bartlett with his Triumph, both machine and rider in full sporting rig

C. Sgonina, known as the 'Welsh Wizard' despite his Italian-sounding name, leaves the line with his potent Sgonina Special at the Margam Park Speed Trials in 1922. White sweaters were fashionable wear at this time

This Excelsior rider, cigarette limply dangling from his lips, seems to scorn the difficulties of High Oak Hill on the Victory Cup Trial. Hall, Hawkins and Walker were the Excelsior riders on this occasion and they received high praise for their gallant efforts on this very tough course with their 'miniature' (147cc) machines, 17 March 1923

Despite the fact that this bike wears the same trade plates (002 OB) as did the machine in the previous picture, it is not the same machine nor the same rider. This rider favours a pipe tightly clenched between his teeth as he copes with a lengthy watersplash in the MC & AC Team Trials on 28 April 1923

'I will lift up mine eyes to the hills from whence I hope 'cometh my help'. As in the picture on p. 112 this is an identical Villiers-engined Excelsior wearing the same trade plates and carries a pillion rider up this stiff gradient in a 1923 trial

Bert Denly, a famous name in Brooklands motor cycle racing and long associated with Nortons, is seen here with his Norton outfit against the background of the Vickers sheds in 1925

Light-hearted sport this, for it is motor cycling football and the ball may be discerned just in front of the machine heading towards the goal in the centre

Two Cottons and a Scott are prominent in this shot of the start of a grasstrack event, c. 1928. The informality of these events is obvious

INDEX

Illustrations are indicated by italic type.